AF211656

ALEXANDER HOLT

SUPER MEMORY

The Essential Guide to Enhancing Your Memory, Learn Effective Techniques and Ways to Sharpen Your Mind and Improve Your Memory

Descrierea CIP a Bibliotecii Naționale a României
ALEXANDER HOLT
   SUPER MEMORY. The Essential Guide to Enhancing Your Memory, Learn Effective Techniques and Ways to Sharpen Your Mind and Improve Your Memory / Alexander Holt. –
Bucharest: Editura My Ebook, 2020
   ISBN 978-606-983-599-9

ALEXANDER HOLT

SUPER MEMORY

**The Essential Guide to Enhancing Your Memory,
Learn Effective Techniques and Ways to Sharpen
Your Mind and Improve Your Memory**

My Ebook Publishing House
Bucharest, 2020

TABLE OF CONTENTS

INTRODUCTION

Want to become a more effective and productive version of you?

The way to do it is to strengthen your mind. By strengthening your brain, you can improve your ability to do *everything* else.

After all, its your brain that you use in order to solve problems, make decisions, and plan for the future. If you are stuck in a rut and if you are failing to get the results you want from life, then it's probably time to take a look at yourself and to try making a change.

When you change yourself, you change the limits of what's possible.

The next question: what to upgrade? A great place to start is with your memory.

By enhancing your memory, you'll be able to improve your ability to learn and store new information. That means you'll be able to add to your skill set, bulk up your resume, and gain new abilities that could help you to land the job of your dreams.

You'll remember names at parties, quote movies, and more. ALL of this can be learned, and in this book you will find out precisely *how* to learn it and what to do with all that knowledge.

Are you ready to unlock the full potential of your brain?

CHAPTER 1

NEUROPLASTICITY AND THE SCIENCE
OF LEARNING

If you want to boost your memory and brain power, then a great place to start is by understanding how your brain works, so that you can "hack" it.

In essence then, it is useful to think of your brain as a giant web of interconnected nodes. These "nodes" are your brain cells – also called neurons – and each one represents a different sensation, memory, thought, or action.

These neurons are arranged roughly into brain regions that have particular roles. For instance, your visual cortex is the brain region that is primarily responsible for your vision. Should you stimulate a neuron in this area using an electrode, then you would see a point of light appear in your field of vision corresponding with that neuron.

Likewise, if you were to stimulate a region of neurons in the hippocampus – the brain region primarily associated with memories – then you might experience some old memories in vivid detail.

These experiments aren't hypothetical – they have been carried out by researchers. They work because the brain is electrical and neurons work by carrying electrical signals called "action potentials."

An action potential occurs when a neuron reaches a certain threshold and then "fires" by sending an electrical current from its soma (cell body) down a tail called an axon. This signal will then usually travel to nearby neurons across a gap called a synapse to their input terminals called "dendrites."

If those neurons are excited enough by this stimulation, they too will then fire and carry the message on further down the axon.

This way, a thought or sensation will spread across the network, lighting up all relevant areas.

When you create a new memory or have a new experience, this will result in the creation of new neurons and new connections.

This is what we call "brain plasticity" and it essentially tells us that the brain is capable of growing and changing shape like a muscle. The more you use specific brain areas, the more those areas increase in size.

And the more skills and knowledge you gain, the more your brain *in general* will grow and change shape!

Plasticity is predicated on one rule that can be represented with a simple maxim:

"Neurons that fire together, wire together."

What this means, is that if two neurons are repeatedly used at the same time, they will gradually form new connections. This is why it's so easy to say the alphabet in order – because those neurons have formed a network that mean you can go directly from a to b to c. This is also how we learn dance routines, and it's why we form "associations" between different events and memories.

If you try to learn something new then, you will do so by creating new neurons and new connections between those neurons. X does Y and E = F. Likewise, you will create episodic memories from everything that happens during your day, which will be comprised of networks of sights, smells, emotions, and things that happened.

The more you make the effort to recall the things that happened or things you tried to learn, the more the corresponding neurons will "fire together" and the stronger the connections that will form. This is why rehearsing something makes it easier to recall.

If your brain deems something to be important enough that has happened during the day, then it will "move" those memories from your short term memory to your long term memory. We now think that this happens during sleep.

This is when the brain "consolidates" memories by moving them from the hippocampus to the cortex. This isn't an area of neuroscience that is yet fully understood, but this is the basic premise. In order for neurons to grow and connect, the brain needs to be highly plastic. Specific neurotransmitters (brain hormones) get produced that can help to support this growth, such as brain derived neurotrophic factor and dopamine.

Neurotransmitters – which are released at the axon terminal during an action potential – can also help to add emotional significance and weight to a particular memory or experience.

Cortisol for example is the "stress hormone" and makes us feel anxious, while also making an event seem particularly pertinent. Serotonin is the "feel good" hormone, and dopamine is the "reward hormone." These chemicals all play key roles in modulating the way we react to outside events.

CHAPTER 2

APPLYING NEUROSCIENCE
TO SMARTER LEARNING

Now that you broadly understand the basics of neuroscience, how can you apply this in practice by using different approaches to learning? Here are some examples.

Spaced Learning

Spaced learning is a very interesting approach to learning that has been shown in studies to be more effective than other approaches.

The general idea, is that you break up your learning into periods of revision and then short breaks. By doing this, you can effectively allow your neurons a 'cool down period' so that they aren't holding any residual charge (their resting potential).

This in turn means that when you then go back to revision, it is as though you are starting a *new* training session and this repetition is more effective than a single prolonged bout of learning. The result is that you actually learn much more, much more quickly.

Emotion

Our brains are designed in such a way that we retain bits of information that might be useful to our survival. We've seen how this works in regards to neurotransmitters. When something happens that is extremely stressful, exciting, or pleasurable, we produce large amounts of hormones and these help us form stronger connections in the brain.

Dopamine for instance – released when we think we are about to be rewarded – will upregulate the production of brain derived neurotrophic factor.

That's why you can probably remember the last argument you had but not what you had for dinner last week. That's also why it's so hard to remember who was Prime Minister in 1934 for that History exam; dry bits of data are boring and have no emotional aspect to them so it's incredibly tricky to seer it into our minds.

Our job then, is to try and make these boring facts and figures into things that seem more exciting, interesting, and relevant to us.

Better yet, we should try to make the actual *act* of learning rewarding and fun.

Here are some examples of how you can do just that:

Watching Education: How can a teacher make any lesson less boring and control a rowdy class? Simple: put a video on. It doesn't matter that the video is the same topic as whatever they were struggling to teach the simple fact is that video is much more stimulating and much better at holding our attention than just reading or just looking at something at something on a blackboard. If you are trying to learn something and finding it boring then, why not see if there's a YouTube video on the topic?

The reason this works is the emotion. When we see people talking, hear music, and get to watch things happening, it triggers a more emotional response, helping us to form more concrete memories.

Multitasking: Learning on its own may be boring, but if you can do it at the same time as something more interesting you'll at least have more stimulation to keep you going and you'll be able to save time. An example of this could be flicking through a text book while running on a treadmill, or listening to an audio tape while playing a computer game on mute.

This isn't so effective at increasing the strength of the memories but can be useful as a way to improve your motivation – so that you spend more time learning than you otherwise could bring yourself too.

Create Something: Another great option is to try creating something as part of your learning process. A great example of this might be to write a blog that recounts all the information you're learning or write a book, or you could even make an app!

This is a great strategy because you will reinforce what you're learning as you write it down. At the same time, if you create a useful enough resource then you'll be able to offer that to others and possibly even earn from it (and you can use the resource yourself to recap).

Writing a book or an article is a particularly effective method, as it draws on something that we call The Feynman method. This is a learning technique that involves reading something, learning as much as you can, and then trying to succinctly explain that concept to someone else. If you can't *easily* explain what you've learned, then you go back and try again.

Make it a Game: This might sound like something un-fun your Mum would try to get you to do in order to keep your room tidier, but there are ways you can turn learning into a fun game. Get more creative than just 'quiz' and think instead about how you can create a board game or something else actually enjoyable out of what you're learning.

Find the Angle That Appeals to You: We all have particular interests and hobbies, and we all decide whether or not something is relevant to us based on whether it applies to these or to part of our careers. The problem with learning maths is often that it doesn't seem to apply to your everyday life and it's common to hear people moaning about how they never use the math skills they learned in school.

In reality though, Maths applies to countless careers and interests

- whether it's architecture where you'll benefit from being able to calculate angles and areas, whether it's physics and space, or whether it's programming.

Love computer games? Well with Maths you can make your own. The same goes for History, for English and for every other topic - it will relate to the things you love in at least some respect.

Even if you can't find that angle naturally you can always force it. So say you are trying to get your kid to learn about history and won't engage with it. Find a TV program or game that they love and then explain to them how it was based on history - or how living in that time would have been just like living in an action movie.

Trying to teach a kid who loves Sonic the Hedgehog about physics? Then try discussing with them the physics of running that fast, whether it would be possible and what would happen to your body if you did.

Nootropics

Nootropics are 'smart drugs' which are increasingly becoming popular as a way to enhance the brain. These work normally by increasing the availability of certain neurotransmitters by blocking transporters or by mimicking their effects.

Caffeine is an example of a nootropic which works by blocking A1 receptors and thus reducing the effectiveness of adenosine while also increasing dopamine and norepinephrine. Piracetam meanwhile is a more 'underground' nootropic that is believed to aid memory by increasing the amount of acetylcholine in the brain.

Ultimately, these work to make you feel more alert and aware and this in turn makes the brain store more information.

Unfortunately, there are risks involved with using smart drugs – some users report that Piracetam gives them brain fog for instance and the mechanism of action is not fully understood.

Another issue is that the interplay between nootropics, neurotransmitters, hormones, metabolism, and more is extremely complex.

For example, you can't just increase dopamine (the reward hormone that supports learning) without also raising cortisol and adrenaline. This makes you more anxious and suppresses your immune system and digestion! It can even damage sleep, which would actually *negatively* affect your memory in the long run.

Better then, is to simply boost your neurotransmitters through a healthy diet. Consuming eggs for instance will give you a supply of choline which the brain uses to *make* acetylcholine.

Likewise, omega 3 fatty acid can improve communication between brain cells by improving cell membrane permeability – this may also then increase recall. Zinc has been demonstrated in studies to play an important role in brain plasticity.

CHAPTER 3

MIND MAPS, MEMORY PALACES, AND OTHER MEMORY TECHNIQUES

The above techniques can all help you to find learning more interesting, and to prime your brain to better receive the information you give it. In this chapter, we're going to look at some of the actual methods you can use to *input* that data.

Here are the best learning, revision, and memorization strategies for boosting your recall.

The "Sheet Technique"

The Sheet Technique essentially means cramming everything you need to know onto one sheet. The benefit of this is that you can then look in just one place in order to revise and test yourself and that you can carry it everywhere with you –

thus revising while you're eating or even seeing a man about a dog.

It certainly feels more manageable in that format too. Furthermore, it's not just having it on a sheet that's helpful but the act of writing it out again and again

So, take your subject, let's say sandwiches. First of all, read all your notes from throughout the year on sandwiches and summarize them as best you can across a few pages. Don't write down anything you already know or ideas for essay answers – these are just the hard facts, the things you need to remember

Now, throughout the course of two or three more attempts, you need to narrow this down more and more using shorter and shorter short-hand to jog your memory without needing reams of writing. The aim here is to get it on one side of A4 paper so that you can simply look down and have all the knowledge in front of you.

Once you've got to this stage you should find that you've already absorbed a lot of facts and dates without even trying to. Now highlight the key dates and facts that you want to jump out at you and start testing yourself from the sheet.

You can carry this everywhere and absently mindedly test yourself while doing other things.

Now with just one sheet in hand it should take no more than a few hours of casual recital to learn everything you need to know. You can utilize not only your semantic memory, but also your visual memory as you attempt to picture the sheet. You can also add sketches, highlights, bold text and other elements that will help the layout to stick in your mind.

With just one page to learn, the amount of work is significantly less.

Mind Maps

In terms of how you should lay out all this information on a single page, mind maps can be extremely useful.

Mind maps are diagrams that link multiple ideas on a single page in the structure of a 'web'. Here you will have a main topic, which will then be broken down into multiple smaller topics all interconnected by lines that show the relationships between these ideas.

If you're looking for a tool that can help you to build beautiful and functional mind maps quickly and easily, then consider the iOS app "Mindly."

The mind map is a tool that has in fact been used for centuries and which has proven highly effective at improving the retention of new ideas and topics. But why?

The Brain Likes Context

The first benefit of mind maps, is that they provide you with context. When you write down a new idea or subject on a mind map, you will do so by finding the correct place to put it and then showing the relationship it has with other ideas via the use of arrows and connecting lines.

What this does then, is to connect all the *related* ideas.

So, if you were to make a mind map of types of sea creatures for instance, you might place one type of fish under a particular category denoting its genus.

With it, would be all the other types of fish that were related to it and perhaps it might also be under a heading showing the fish's habitat, or how it reproduces.

What this does, is to surround the information with extra details any of which can help to 'jog' your memory. When you're then sitting in an exam, you might not be able to think of the name of the fish immediately but if you can remember the surrounding items – the related fish, the genus, the habitat – then this might be enough to help you come to the answer.

Cross-Modality

Our brain also has something of a preference for visual stimuli and will often find this easier to remember. The great thing about mind maps is that you can combine images with text, color and even sounds and videos if you're using an app.

As a result, even if you can't immediately remember the name of that fish, you might be able to remember where it was on the mind map and the image it was next to – and again that might be enough to 'nudge' you in the correct direction.

This is also why learning from a television program is more effective when it comes to ingesting lots of information (as well as the discussed fact that this helps to increase your emotional response and attention).

When you watch a documentary about a topic, you learn not only from the content, but from the music, the imagery, and more. This creates more "in roads" for accessing the information you need.

Mindly unfortunately does not allow you to add images and video, but what you can do is to print out your work and then annotate and draw on it.

Organization

Finally, if nothing else, a mind map enables you to organize information in a logical manner. This in turn makes it easier to retrieve that information and also means that you can fit it all conveniently on one page for quick reference.

So now we've addressed how to lay out your revision so that it's more manageable how do you actually get it from the sheet of paper and etched into your mind?

Mnemonics

Mnemonics can be helpful. These are "tricks" to jog your memory, such as acronyms and rhymes. And we can take this further – by creating mini-stories linking names or dates together. For example, in psychology I had to remember that a researcher Frankenhause did an experiment to test if there was a gender effect on a recent finding.

Firstly, I only had to remember that he was finding a gender effect as I'd previously learned the context and I'd be able to remember it being under the relevant study on my sheet. I could remember the outcome as that was interesting – it was just the name and the date that I needed to link to this information. So, I controversially used 'Frankenhause' by thinking of a 'house wife'.

It barely makes sense but it's controversial and related to genders so it sticks in my mind (an unpopular example but it's the one that springs to mind!). Again, an emotional context really helps to memorize this, as does actually picturing a house wife.

The date was 1987 – the year I was born – and I'm pretty sure something similar to 'Frankenhause' means hospital in German. Like many of you I was born in a hospital and this was enough of a connection for me to remember it.

The weirder and more nonsensical it is, often the better you'll be at remembering it later.

That's not what the true Memory Masters do ,however. Although they do often use a story they prefer to 'visualize' that story as our sensory memory is often more reliable. The story will be made up of very unique image, each one tying to the last.

This method is particularly good for remembering long lists of objects – say a shopping list – as they're easier to visualise. Here you create a visual image tying together two consecutive images. So for Monkey, Brick, Cleaner, Squirrel you might imagine a monkey bashing himself with a brick – now think about that in detail and really drink it in/enjoy the image for a good minute or two.

Now the next one, a brick being feather dusted by a cleaner for example. Funny or bizarre images work best – make up your own!

So how can this apply to numbers or dates? Well here 'Memory Masters' use a clever trick, utili\ing a visual 'code' based on rhyme and use these universally across images. For example one can be 'bun' or 'sun' and two can be 'stew' or 'loo'... you get it. Now you have to incorporate these into your images and hey presto, easy to remember dates.

Memory Palaces and the Method of Loci

Want to take this concept one step further even? Then you could try to create an entire "memory palace."

Made famous by the recent BBC series *Sherlock*, this technique involves creating an imaginary location and then filling it with things you want to recall. (That location could also be real and based on a memory).

Once again, the aim is to use images that are extremely vivid and easy to recall, and to then "link them" in some way to a particular spot in your home. For instance, the front door might have one image linked with it, while your hallway might have another.

This technique and similar ones have been used by indigenous tribes and early man for hundreds of years. More specifically, they have used a technique referred to as the "method of loci." This is a slight twist on the notion of the memory palace, that instead uses a 'route' that the person or tribe takes often.

In your case, that might mean the route to work for instance, or the way to the nearest shop. You then place your memories at landmarks along this route, so that they prompt different ideas.

This way, you could go on a long walk and then tell a long story or convey huge amounts of information by being prompted by the landmarks along the way.

Tying this information up as stories also helped them to "hack" their memories in this way.

This strategy is one that could help to store large amounts of data as a culture, during a time before books, computers, or the internet.

All they needed was their brains and good stories!

CHAPTER 4

ACCELERATED LEARNING AND PUTTING IT ALL TOGETHER

At this point, you now have a huge amount of information regarding memory. You know the basics of how your brain works, you understand some of the most advanced strategies for making the most from it, and more.

But now the big question: what do you do with all this memory power?

For example: what do you do with the method of loci or memory palace? How does this make you a smarter, more successful individual?

One option is to use it to memorize passages of text. Need to deliver a speech from memory? Wish you could reel off long quotes from books? Using the method of loci, you can achieve these feats and more.

Of course, many of the techniques such as the sheet technique, mind maps, and YouTube videos are also extremely useful for students – as can be the method of loci.

But what about the high flying executive? What about the average office worker? What about someone who just wants to get more from life as an adult?

You might think that you never really use your memory, and that as such, you don't need to develop these kinds of skills.

But that's the wrong way to look at it. You don't have a great memory right now *because* you don't use it. If you *start* using it, then you will find that you can increase your memory hugely.

Because here's the real secret to memory: the more you use it, the better it becomes!

This is because learning actually increases the amount of brain derived neurotrophic factor that you produce, along with other chemicals such as nerve growth factor. In short, the more you learn, the better your brain becomes at learning.

The more you remember, the better you become at remembering!

And imagine if you could just *effortlessly* remember everyone's names at events. Imagine if you could learn without even trying – and then impress people with quotes and facts.

This is what happens when you make the effort.

So how do you practice? Simple: you keep learning like a student. You keep teaching yourself new and exciting things.

As you do this, you will find that your brain becomes better at learning AND you become better at using these techniques. More to the point though, by learning new subjects and skills, you'll boost your own performance and success.

Rather than wait for your boss to send you on a learning course, why not enhance your own resume with new skills and qualifications, then find a better paid job?

By combining constant learning and improved memory techniques, you'll be using something called "accelerated learning." Here are some more strategies that can help.

Speed Reading

The idea behind speed reading is an incredibly useful one - to be able to flick through the pages of a book as quickly as possible and absorb all the information would make you a master of most subjects. It would also be massively useful for a variety of jobs and studying. Read on (speedily or otherwise) to find out how to do it.

Basically when we count or read we have to 'sound out' the words or numbers in our brain in order to register them; the basic idea behind speed reading then is that you learn to flick your eyes across text and take it in without needing to make the sounds. 'Absorbing' the information without repeating it. The idea is that by making the sounds in your head you are slowing yourself down.

Thus to read more quickly you need to sound these out faster, or preferably not at all. For a large unreasonable fee, 'Gurus' teach their book buyers/course attendees to do this by practicing running their eyes across text then testing themselves several times a day until they good at reading without sounding out the words (I'm a sandwich guru).

If you want to try it then get yourself a non-fiction text book and sit it on your lap. Now run your eyes across the text (you can trace the words with your fingers if you like) but try not to form the words with your inner voice, instead try to 'absorb the meaning' but don't put too much effort in.

Now after you've read a page or so try searching your mind for certain questions - what was the section about? Who was the author? What is the average weight for a male sheep?? At first you should find you're shit at it (or you're a freak). But practice daily and you shuold find yourself improving. Let me know how you do.

This has lead to mixed reports and it appears that it works for some and not others. Even the supporters however recommend that you don't try and use it for novels as you just don't absorb as much information.

This does however highlight the interesting link between language and thought. Studies have regularly shown that concepts that don't exist in the language of a culture cannot be grasped by those who speak it. More interestingly, different languages have been shown to solve problems more quickly than others.

Another strategy you can use that may make things easier, is an app called Spreeder. Spreeder essentially lets you paste any amount of text into a box and will then display all the words in rapid succession, keeping them on the screen barely long enough for you to absorb them.

You can change the precise speed and you'll get an estimated amount of time taken. Try it at Spreeder.com.

The First 20 Hours

The First 20 Hours is the name of a book by Josh Kaufman that puts forward a powerful learning technique for gaining new skills and abilities.

That technique essentially involves trying to create or achieve something with the knowledge you are acquiring. Too often, we will approach an idea or topic with no real idea of where we intend to go with it.

This in turn means we often have no idea where to start. We might try to learn programming for instance by just "learning programming." This is far too broad a subject and is overwhelming.

Instead then, you should aim to learn *enough* to achieve something specific. That might mean that you learn how to make a particular app you have in mind in this case.

By doing that, you will help to structure your learning, you'll add more motivation and emotional intent, and you'll be able to expand your learning as you go. This is *far* more effective.

Combine this with online courses and certificates, and you can reignite your capacity for learning, jumpstart your career, and boost your brain power significantly.

Prospective Memory

At this point, you understand the way the brain works and you have a lot of different ideas regarding the best ways to enhance memory. To recap, you need to improve your sleep and nutrition, make learning more interesting, use mind maps, and practice using the method of loci and Feynman technique.

Using these techniques, you can begin to learn more topics more quickly, you can memorize passages of text, and much more. In short, you can start to become a more efficient and effective version of yourself, like Eddie Mora in limitless!

But before you get too carried away, you might notice that you still get accused of a bad memory – of being absent minded even.

You tell people you're training to boost your memory and they just laugh…

You?? You couldn't even remember to get milk!

The truth is that "remembering to get milk" and being able to memorize a pack of cards (for which you might use the method of loci and number encoding) are two *very* different things.

The issue with milk is that it comes down to "remembering to remember."

This has far more to do with your awareness and your attention than it does to conventional storage and retrieval. You *know* that you should get milk, and if asked "what do you need to do today" then you could answer. The problem is *thinking* about this before you get home.

This is called "prospective memory" and there are a few ways to enhance it.

Meditation and Mindfulness

One option is to use meditation and mindfulness. Mindfulness means taking more time to be conscious of what you are doing at any given moment and to stop being "in your own head."

A good example of just how distracted we are can be seen when you try this simple experiment: counting how many times you sit down and stand up in a day.

Try and do this today. It's a simple task and yet most people won't remember to count even *once*.

To overcome this limitation, try to practice being more aware and alert at every moment during the day. Ask yourself to think what it is you're doing and what you *should* be doing at every waking moment.

And finally, practice meditation to help thicken your connective tissue and improve your focus.

Flow Charts and Checklists

When engaging in an important task, don't be above using a checklist or flow chart to ensure you follow each step and don't forget anything important. While this might seem like hand- holding, studies show that highly trained professional surgeons make *considerably* fewer mistakes when forced to use a checklist.

While you can do a lot to improve your memory, sometimes it will still be fallible… and there is no harm in doing what you can to support it when it really matters.

CHAPTER 5

FLUID AND CRYSTALIZED INTELLIGENCE

Does boosting your memory increase your intelligence?

In fact… what **is** intelligence? There are plenty of ways to answer that question and all manner of different ways to try and measure it or to try and quantify it.

So far, the term has eluded a complete and comprehensive definition but one important distinction that we can generally agree on, is the difference between fluid intelligence and crystalized intelligence.

How Can Intelligence be Fluid?

When you think of someone intelligent you know, you might think of someone who knows an awful lot about history, politics and science. Perhaps you're picturing someone who is a font of all knowledge and who is constantly impressing you with different facts and ideas.

Perhaps this is your objective for trying to learn as much as possible and boost your memory.

But is this person really *intelligent* or are they in fact just knowledgeable? If you take someone with a low IQ and you spend years teaching them all about history and politics, then they would become a very knowledgeable person. But would that make them any better at math? At reasoning? Or at making smart decisions?

This is the difference between fluid intelligence and crystalized intelligence. Fluid intelligence broadly refers to the ability to think quickly and to come up with solutions to problems and novel ideas.

Meanwhile, crystalized intelligence refers to pure knowledge: this is all about *how much* you know rather than your ability to 'use' that information.

Therefore, boosting memory improves crystalized intelligence, but not necessarily fluid. Though as we'll see, the distinction is a little blurry even here.

Which is Better?

So now you might be wondering what the difference between these two different types of intelligence is and even which one is 'superior'. Would you rather have more fluid intelligence or more crystalized intelligence?

The answer of course is that neither is superior and that each has its uses. What's more, is that it isn't quite as clear cut a definition as you might expect.

One interesting thing to note though is that fluid intelligence tends to be better when we're younger but then decline as we get older. Conversely though, crystalized intelligence is something that *improves* as you age. The older you get, the more time you have to experience things, to read books and to collect knowledge (though your actual recall can deteriorate).

But as we've said is that the distinction isn't perfect. For one, someone with better fluid intelligence might find it *easier* to learn more things. They might also feel more motivated to discover new subjects and they might be able to grasp the meaning of these subjects more than someone who just rote learned them. In this way then, there is a strong correlation between the two types of intelligence meaning that they aren't entirely separate.

Working Memory: The Last Piece of the Puzzle

Of course, fluid intelligence itself can be broken down into many other different types of intelligence. Psychologists like Gardner posit that we have multiple 'types' of intelligence which could all be considered fluid, whereas modular theories of the brain point to the different roles that different brain areas have when it comes to planning, memorizing and using language.

One big predictor of fluid intelligence though is another type of memory that we have yet to consider: the working memory. The working memory is a little like the brain's 'RAM'; it is what allows it to store information temporarily for use during thinking.

If you need to perform mental arithmetic for example, then you will likely need to 'carry over' numbers in your mind while you perform sums and multiplications. This is handled by the working memory.

Likewise, the working memory allows us to store images in our mind's eye (called the 'visospatial scratch-pad') and to remember names and phone numbers (using the 'phonological loop'). It is also closely correlated with attention and our ability to stay fixated on a certain subject.

It's only with repetition and when we view information as being important that it goes on to be transferred to the short term memory and then later the long-term memory for permanent storage. And it is at this point that it begins to contribute to overall 'crystalized intelligence'.

The long term memories seem to be stored by the limbic system and in particular, by the hippocampus. The limbic system is *also* in charge of many of our emotions however and thus it might be that it encourages the storage of information that it views as emotionally 'important'.

Working memory is still memory, but it has nothing to do with recall. It instead has to do with what you can hold in your mind's eye for a given amount of time.

It's your ability to remember a phone number before writing it down for instance, or to memorize the items on a table before someone throws a blanket over them. This is your bottleneck to recall and storage, and also one of your greatest tools for manipulating that information.

So how do you improve this extremely specific form of memory? One of the only methods proven to work is a game/test called the "Dual N-Back Test." This is a test that involves looking for repetitions in numbers and letters that appear on a screen, and hitting a button when you see them.

Dual N-back forces you to hold in your mind all the letters and numbers that have come before, and this way allows you to improve your focus and your working memory. Practicing this is one of the only ways to boost your fluid intelligence, and potentially to enhance your crystalized intelligence as a result.

Abstract Thinking

But to say that fluid intelligence is entirely the result of working memory and attention would be a mistake. It is true that the working memory enhances our ability to focus, to make quick decisions and to juggle information, but it is less involved in the kind of creative thinking that gives rise to novel ideas.

Actually, creativity appears to be the result of having a more relaxed approach to thinking. The general view is that new ideas are only ever created by combining old ideas in unique ways. If you can do this, then you can 'think outside the box' and you can come up with new inventions, stories and creations.

In order to have these kinds of creative thoughts though, it is important to be able to let the mind 'wander', which in turn appears to be closely linked to emotion, as well as to overall connectivity throughout the brain.

What's also true though, is that by having more knowledge, you might actually be better able to recombine that information in new ways. The more 'input' you have, the more 'output' you will be capable of.

Sleep once again plays an important role here too. Sleep well and your REM state will help you to make more indirect connections between different memories and thoughts, thereby helping you to have more original ideas and even solve problems.

CONCLUSION

We would describe all these types of intelligence as 'fluid'. The ability to focus on a task, excellence in a particular area (such as maths) or the ability to come up with novel ideas.

The mechanisms behind these types of thinking are many and not fully understood but by categorizing them as 'fluid', we can at least make the distinction between knowledge and information.

So, what can you do to improve these types of intelligence? What should you do with this information?

One tip is to practice training your working memory if you want to increase your fluid intelligence and to spend some time relaxing and letting your mind wander if you want to come up with new ideas.

And through it all, keep on learning. Because not only will this help you to come up with new ideas and work in tandem with your fluid intelligence, but it is also the type of intelligence that will stay with you long into old age!

This is the ultimate "memory hack" and also the ultimate life hack!

Printed by Libri Plureos GmbH in Hamburg, Germany